RECORDER ENSEMBLE
First Collection

Soprano ❧ Alto ❧ Tenor ❧ Bass

Printed with support from the Waldorf Curriculum Fund

Published by
Waldorf Publications
38 Main Street
Chatham, New York 12037

Title: *Recorder Ensemble, First Collection: Soprano, Alto, Tenor, Bass*
Author/arranger: Steve Bernstein
Director of Publications: Patrice Maynard
Design/cover: Shellie Pomeroy www.mystudiodesigns.com
Layout: Ann Erwin

ISBN#: 978-1-936367-46-7

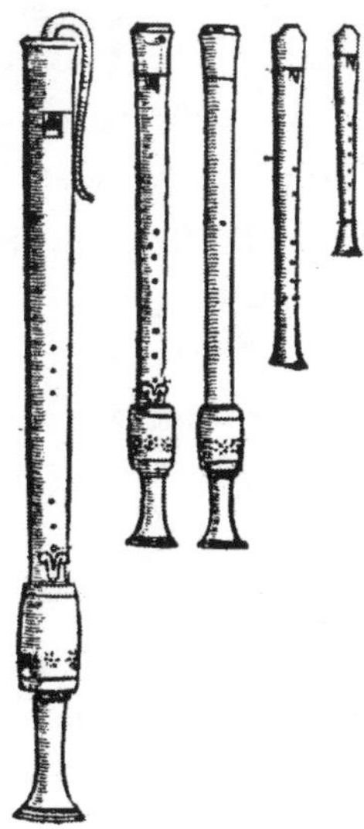

Songs by
Praetorius, Morley, Valentine and J.S. Bach
and traditional tunes from
Scotland, Italy, England and more.

arranged for recorder ensemble by Steve Bernstein

It was in 2003 when I began teaching music at the Mountain Laurel Waldorf School in New Paltz, NY. I had listened to the school's recorder ensemble and was amazed at the skill that these elementary and middle school children possessed when playing their recorders. After a decade of directing this talented group, I am still amazed!

This book was written for recorder ensemble directors who, like myself, are looking for recorder arrangements written in four parts (SATB) for intermediate and advanced players. My understanding of "intermediate" is a player who knows the fingerings and can read music reasonably well. From my experience, students in the fifth grade and older are ready for the level of music found in this book.

In this collection you will find traditional Scottish, English and Welsh folk songs, music from the Renaissance and Barique periods, and a couple of my own compositions. Most of the arrangements are in four parts (SATB), with a few written for larger ensembles featuring additional alto or tenor parts. There are also three trios (ATB).

The scores presented in this book are either one page or two facing pages, making the scores easy for conducting. With each system bracketed, students will find it easy to follow the different parts, although some may want to highlight their parts.

As the book progresses, the tunes become more challenging as dynamics and slurring are introduced. Use these techniques as you need depending on your group's playing level. Recorders do not possess a large dynamic range due to intonation issues, so sometimes it may be necessary to subtract players from particular sections to achieve pianissimo or add players to achieve fortissimo. Slurring is a wonderful effect. Some of the tunes have detailed slurring instructions, especially "The Black Nag," where triplets abound. In Valentine's "Rondeau" I left the slurring out to give the conductor some latitude in deciding which groups will slur and which will not. Generally, I don't have the basses slur because I am looking for more definition in their phrases.

I have been very fortunate to have had the opportunity to conduct some really fine-sounding ensembles at Mountain Laurel. All of the pieces contained herein are tunes I have taught to my recorder ensembles with wonderful results. It is my hope that these arrangements will be challenging and fun for all who play and teach the recorder.

Sincerely,
Steve Bernstein
July 2013

Thank you to the students, parents, faculty and administration at Mountain Laurel for their enthusiastic support over the years. Most of all I want to thank Shellie Pomeroy for her patience, her artistic eye, and her willingness to help me in this endeavor. Above all, Shellie, thank you for your friendship.

TABLE OF CONTENTS

1. All through the Night (*Trad. Welsh*)

2. For the Beauty of the Earth (*C. Kocher/F. Pierpont*)

3. Ye Banks and Braes (*Trad. Scottish*)

4. Lauda (*15th Century Italian*)

5. Courante (*M. Praetorius*)

6. Volte (*M. Praetorius*)

7. Brandenburg Concerto No. 1 in F major Menuetto (*J.S. Bach*)*

8. Brandenburg Concerto No. 1 in F major Trio (*J.S. Bach*)

9. Orchestral Suite No. 2 in B minor Menuet (*J.S. Bach*)

10. Orchestral Suite No. 2 in B minor Rondeau (*J.S. Bach*)

11. The Black Nag (*Trad. English*)

12. Rondeau (*R. Valentine*)

13. April Is in My Mistress' Face (*T. Morley*)

14. Musketeer Minuet (*S. Bernstein*)

15. Mr. Neel's Circus (*S. Bernstein*)

*After playing the Menuetto in Brandenburg Concerto No. 1,
turn the page and play the Trio, then repeat the Menuetto.

Fingering Chart

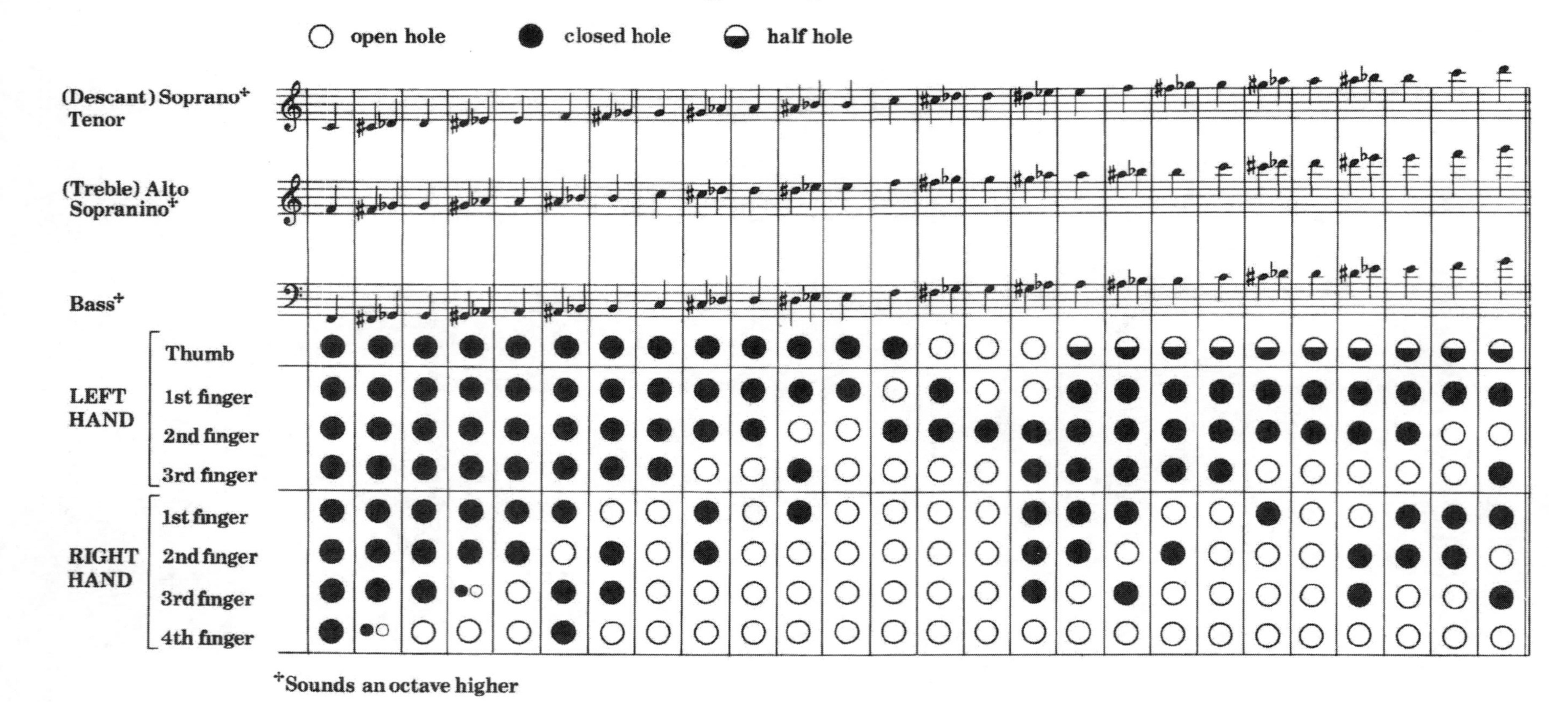

+Sounds an octave higher

All through the Night

Moderato

Trad. Welsh
Arr. by Steve Bernstein

For the Beauty of the Earth

Moderato

Tune (Dix) Conrad Kocher (1786–1872)
Text Folliott Pierpoint (1835–1917)
Arr. by Steve Bernstein

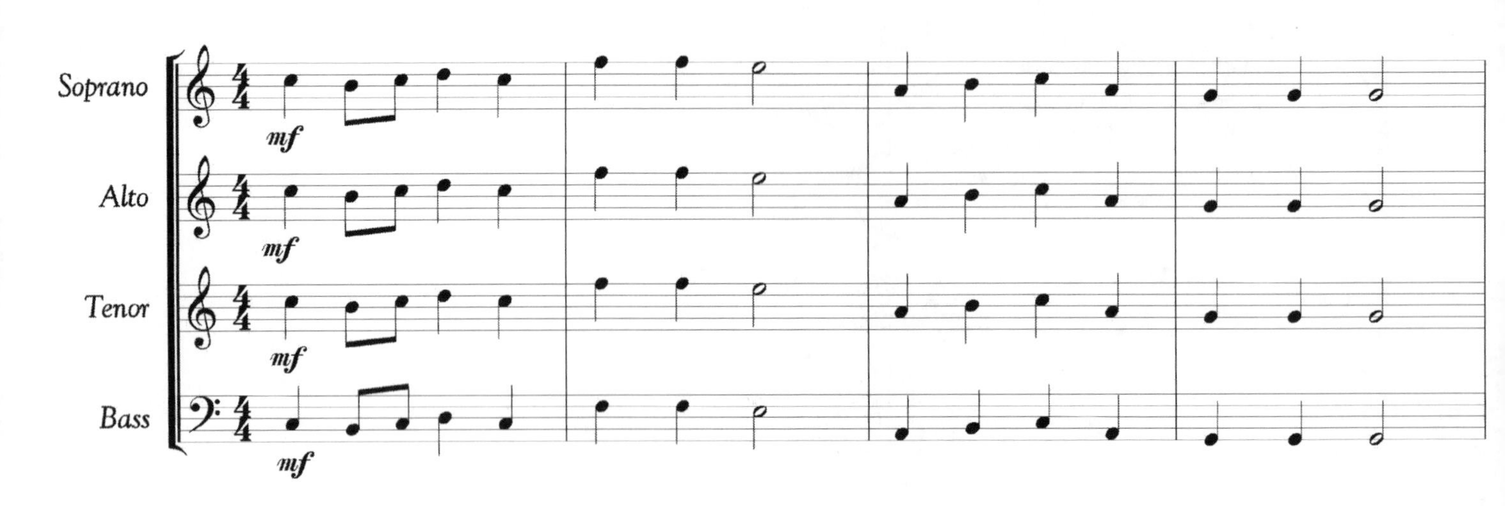

13
17
21
rit.
conducted
rit.
conducted
rit.
conducted
rit.
conducted

Ye Banks and Braes

Waltz

Trad. Scottish
Arr. by Steve Bernstein

Lauda

Largemente

15th Century Italian
Arr. by Steve Bernstein

Courante

Allegro

Michael Praetorius (c. 1571–1621)
Dances from Terpsichore
Arr. for recorders by Steve Bernstein

32
p
p
p
p
40
cresc. poco a poco
mp
cresc. poco a poco
mp
cresc. poco a poco
mp
cresc. poco a poco
mp
mf
mf
mf
mf
48
f
f
f
f
ff
ff
ff
ff
tr
56
tr
ff
ff
ff
ff
slight rit.
slight rit.
slight rit.
slight rit.

Volte

(for 5 parts)

Michael Praetorius (c. 1571–1621)
Dances from Terpsichore
Arr. for recorders by Steve Bernstein

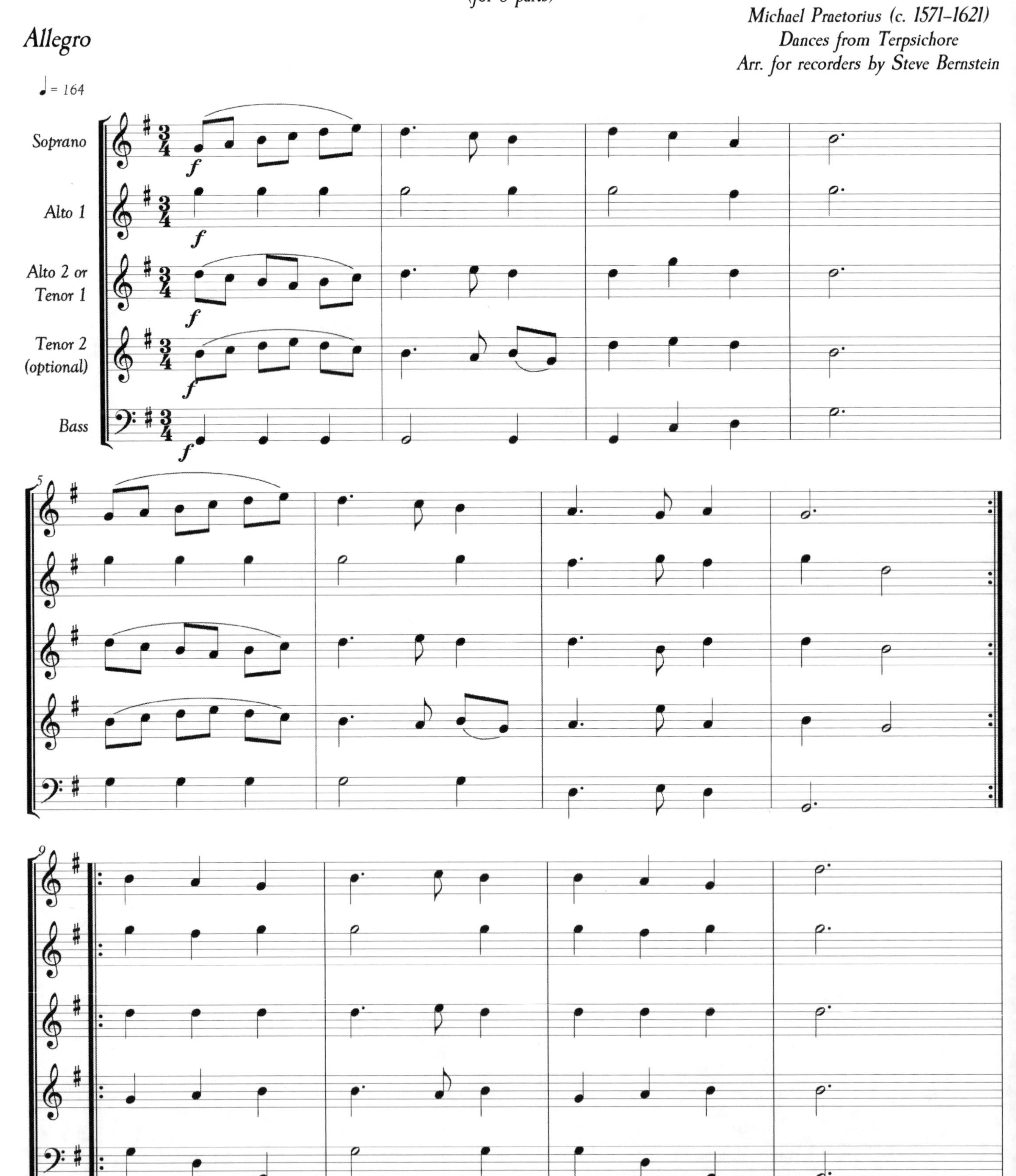

13
17
21

Brandenburg Concerto No. 1 in F major

Menuetto

J.S. Bach (1685–1750)
Arr. for recorders by Steve Bernstein

14
Soprano
Alto 1
Alto 2
Tenor 1
Tenor 2
Bass
19
23
rit. on repeat
rit. on repeat
rit. on repeat
rit. on repeat
rit. on repeat
rit. on repeat
1.
2.
to Trio

Brandenburg Concerto No. 1 in F major

Trio

J.S. Bach (1685–1750)
Arr. for recorders by Steve Bernstein

Orchestral Suite No. 2 in B minor

Menuet

J.S. Bach (1685–1750)
Arr. for recorders by Steve Bernstein

Orchestral Suite No. 2 in B minor

Rondeau

J.S. Bach (1685–1750)
Arr. by Steve Bernstein

27
Alto 1
Alto 2
(Tenor 2)
Tenor
Bass
34
41
48

The Black Nag

Jig

Trad. English
Arr. by Steve Bernstein

24
1.
2.
3
3
mp
mp
30
mp
mp
cresc.
cresc.
cresc.
cresc.
34
ff
ff
ff
ff
risoluto
risoluto
risoluto
risoluto
fff
fff
fff
fff

Rondeau

Allegro

Robert Valentine (1671–1747)
Arr. by Steve Bernstein

24
mf
mf
mf
30
mf
mp
mp
mp
mp
cresc.
cresc.
cresc.
cresc.
mf
mf
mf
mf
36
f
f
f
f
42

April Is in My Mistress' Face

(First Book of Ayres 1594)

Moderato

♩= 112

Thomas Morley (1557–1602)
Arr. by Steve Bernstein

18
p mf
p
p mf
p
mf
25
p
mf
mf
p mf
p mf
p
32
mf
rall.
p
rall.
p
rall.
p
rall.
p

The Musketeer Minuet

21
mf
mf
mf
mf
26
mp
mp
mp
mp
31
1.
mp
mp
mf
mf
mf
mf
36
2.
cresc.
cresc.
cresc.
cresc.
D.C. al Fine
f
f
f
f

Mr. Neel's Circus

11
15
1.
19
2.
mf
f
ff
fff

Steve Bernstein is director of the recorder ensemble at
Mountain Laurel Waldorf School in New Paltz, NY.
He arranges traditional folk melodies, Renaissance and Baroque music,
and popular tunes for recorders in four parts: soprano, alto, tenor and bass.
Some of his arrangements have additional percussion and guitar parts.

For additional
Recorder Arrangements
contact:
Steve Bernstein
sbernstein1@hvc.rr.com

www.recorderensemblemusic.com

Made in the USA
Las Vegas, NV
29 April 2024